Dear Parent:

Buckle up! You are about to join your child on a very exciting journey. The destination? Independent reading!

Road to Reading will help you and your child get there. The program offers books at five levels, or Miles, that accompany children from their first attempts at reading to successfully reading on their own. Each Mile is paved with engaging stories and delightful artwork.

Getting Started
For children who know the alphabet and are eager to begin reading
• easy words • fun rhythms • big type • picture clues

Reading With Help
For children who recognize some words and sound out others with help
• short sentences • pattern stories • simple plotlines

Reading On Your Own
For children who are ready to read easy stories by themselves
• longer sentences • more complex plotlines • easy dialogue

First Chapter Books
For children who want to take the plunge into chapter books
• bite-size chapters • short paragraphs • full-color art

Chapter Books
For children who are comfortable reading independently
• longer chapters • occasional black-and-white illustrations

There's no need to hurry through the Miles. Road to Reading is designed without age or grade levels. Children can progress at their own speed, developing confidence and pride in their reading ability no matter what their age or grade.

So sit back and enjoy the ride—every Mile of the way!

For the Glucklings,
Alan and Max
B.B.

For Liz, Bonnie, and Elise—
dance troupe of the imagination
D.B.

Library of Congress Cataloging-in-Publication Data
Bottner, Barbara.
Marsha is only a flower / by Barbara Bottner ; illustrated by
Denise Brunkus.
    p. cm.— (Road to reading. Mile 3)
Summary: All Lulu can think about is her solo role in the ballet
recital, until she realizes that her younger sister is in danger.
ISBN 0-307-26330-4 (pbk) — ISBN 0-307-46330-3 (GB)
[1. Ballet Fiction.   2. Sisters Fiction.   3. Behavior Fiction.]
I. Brunkus, Denise, ill. II. Title. III. Series.
PZ7. B6586Mai 2000
[E]—dc21   99-24650
                                                            CIP

A GOLDEN BOOK • New York
Golden Books Publishing Company, Inc. New York, New York 10106

ISBN: 0-307-26330-4 (pbk)
ISBN: 0-307-46330-3 (GB)
10   9   8   7   6   5   4   3   2

Marsha Is Only a Flower

by Barbara Bottner
illustrated by Denise Brunkus

"Look at me!

I'm a beautiful Princess," Lulu said.

She showed off her ballet costume

for Marsha.

"Someday, if you are lucky,

you might be a Princess, too.

But now you are only a Flower.

The littlest Flower in the whole show."

Lulu began to dance.

"I will show you the steps

for my solo," she said.

Lulu stood on her toes

and twirled.

Then she did a leap.

Marsha watched every step

Lulu made.

"Can you believe how well

I dance?" asked Lulu.

"Loo-loo," was all

Marsha could say.

"Now, show me

your Flower dance!" said Lulu.

Marsha wiggled on the floor.

Then she waved her arms.

"No! No! No!" yelled Lulu.

"Flowers don't wave!"

Marsha's head drooped.

She crawled away.

"Come back here!" cried Lulu.

But Marsha was gone.

Lulu sighed and got back to work.
It took hours and hours
of practice to be a Princess.
Tomorrow, at the ballet recital,
Marsha would see that Lulu
was truly a star.

Backstage the next morning,

Lulu put on her Princess costume.

"I want you to watch me

every single minute

I'm onstage,"

Lulu said to her mother.

"I will watch you and Marsha, too,"

her mother said.

"*Marsha!*

Why watch her?" asked Lulu.

"She is only a Flower."

But Lulu's mother didn't hear her.

She was too busy finding her seat.

Miss Miriam, the teacher,

brought the dancers together.

"Remember," she said,

"when I start to play,

Green Frog, Swan, and Evil Prince

leap onstage.

The Flowers will follow them.

Then it's Lulu's turn to do her solo.

Does everyone understand?"

They all nodded.

Even Marsha.

Then Miss Miriam went

to take her seat at the piano.

As soon as Miss Miriam

was out of sight,

Lulu said, "Don't forget.

Everyone came to see *me*.

The best dancer in the show."

"We are all good dancers," said Swan.

"Just as good as you!" said Green Frog.

"Maybe even better," said Evil Prince.

"You are not bad," said Lulu.

"But I'm the one with the solo."

Down in the pit, Miss Miriam
opened the sheet music.
"Ready? Here we go!"
she shouted.
She hit the first chords.

The blue lights turned purple.

The leaves fluttered.

"Everybody dance!" shouted Lulu.

"This is your cue!"

But nobody moved fast enough for Lulu.

So Lulu pushed Green Frog, Swan,

and Evil Prince onstage.

"It's your cue, too!" she said

to Marsha and the Flowers.

She pushed them onstage.

"Everybody dance together!"

Lulu shouted.

Soon it would be Lulu's turn.

Everyone was waiting for her solo.

And she was ready!

Finally, Miss Miriam played new chords.

Yes! It was time for the Princess.

"Scram, everybody!" Lulu shouted.

"It's my turn!"

Green Frog, Swan, Evil Prince,
and the Flowers danced
into the wings.

At last, Lulu jumped onstage.

The spotlight hit her eyes.

It was so bright!

How did her dance go?

Was it a twirl and then a leap?

Or a leap and then a twirl?

Lulu just stood there.

There were so many eyes
staring at her.
It was such a *big* stage,
she thought.
Nobody was on it.
Except for her.
Alone. All alone.

Miss Miriam played

the Princess song louder!

It was no use.

Lulu couldn't remember her steps.

What was she going to do?

Could she sing?

Could she juggle?

If only she could fly!

Suddenly, Lulu heard a sound.

Everyone was laughing.

Loudly.

Oh, no!

Were they laughing at her?

But then she saw that nobody

was even looking at her.

They were looking at *Marsha!*

They were laughing at *Marsha!*

The littlest Flower

had crawled back onstage.

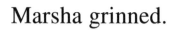

Marsha grinned.

And giggled.

And waved.

Everyone loved Marsha!

For a minute Lulu
loved Marsha, too.

But the minute passed quickly.

"No wonder I can't dance!

You are in my way!"

Lulu hissed to Marsha.

Marsha's head drooped.

She crawled offstage.

33

Once again, the blue lights
turned purple.
The leaves fluttered.
Miss Miriam played the
Princess song again.
Now, Lulu remembered everything.

This time, she stood on her toes
and twirled and twirled.
She made giant leaps
across the stage.
Lulu was the most beautiful
Princess ever!
She never wanted to stop dancing.

But then Lulu saw something.

It was Marsha.

She was crawling toward
the edge of the stage.

She was in the wrong place
for a baby sister!

"Marsha, stop!" shouted Lulu.

But Marsha did not listen.

"*Please!*" begged Lulu.

But Marsha kept crawling.

"Help! Frog! Swan! Prince!"
called Lulu.
But Miss Miriam was playing
too loudly.
Nobody heard Lulu.

Lulu looked out at the audience.

Nobody even saw Marsha.

They were too busy looking at her.

No one was going to help
her baby sister.

Lulu would have to do it herself.

Lulu leaped over to Marsha.

She reached out to grab her.

At last, Green Frog, Swan,

and Evil Prince

saw what was happening.

They ran out to help.

Lulu picked Marsha up.

She twirled her around

as if it was part of her dance.

"Wheee!" giggled Marsha.

Marsha was safe!

But it was too late

for the others to stop.

They were running too fast.

They bumped right into

Lulu and Marsha.

Everyone rolled backstage

like a giant snowball.

The curtain dropped.

The audience shouted,
"Bravo! We want more!"
All the dancers crawled
out from under the curtain.
"They love us," said Green Frog.
"But everything went wrong!"
said Lulu.

Miss Miriam played an encore.

All the dancers bowed.

The audience stood up

and clapped even more.

Lulu beamed.

Backstage, Lulu's mother
hugged Marsha.
"My baby girl was in
her *first* recital!" she said.
Marsha smiled a silly smile.

"What about *me*, *me*, *me*?" asked Lulu.

"Lulu, you were wonderful!

In fact, both of you were wonderful!"

said her mother.

"Both of us?" asked Lulu.

"Both of you!" said her mother.

"Loo-loo!" Marsha said

as she waved her arms at Lulu.

Lulu looked over at her little sister.

"I decided that Princesses love Flowers," said Lulu softly.

"Someday, it will be your turn to be a Princess.

And I am the perfect one to teach you."